# HOW TO ANALYZE SI

## ADVANCED TECHNIQUES FOR READING BODY LANGUAGE & NON-VERBAL COMMUNICATION

### SCOTT COLTER

# TABLE OF CONTENTS

# FREE GIFT

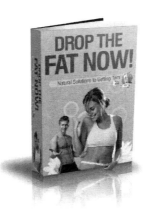

**Drop the Fat Now!**
**Natural Solutions to Getting Trim**

# INTRODUCTION

Most people have heard of body language, but fewer have heard of the term 'kinesics'. Kinesics is the fancy psychological term for body language and is technically defined as the study of facial expressions and gestures.

The basis of kinesics is simple; movement, expression and gesture are all part of communication. They can convey meaning and intent in order to understand other people better. Kinesics is still a nascent science – you won't suddenly become a Machiavellian mind reader by studying it. However, you will start to, on occasion, read and interpret the people around you more successfully by being mindful of small cues – such as body posture – to understand what other people may be feeling.

The allure of kinesics is in it's hidden power. We like to be in control of our own actions and how we present ourselves to other people. The notion that our own body language can betray what we are saying, or that we can pick up on the duplicity of other people is intoxicating.

This is especially true in the workplace or unfamiliar social settings. We all want to give the impression of confidence, calmness and competence but sometimes our body language may undermine us. If you've ever walked away from an interview wondering why you didn't get that job you wanted, or why people don't seem to take to you as quickly as they should, your failure may be due to poor understanding of kinesics. This book aims to solve that!

There are six chapters in this book. The first chapter will take you through the basics of kinesics, informing you about how body language is categorized.

The second chapter will take you through other categorizations of body language that you might hear on occasion, such as haptics and paralanguage.

The third chapter will teach you how to improve your non-verbal communication, by managing stress and being mindful of body language-verbal inconsistencies and much more.

The fourth chapter will help you get to grips with how to make a good first impression and the psychological factors that influence how you are perceived on first appearance.

The fifth chapter will give you a small introduction to some of the cultural differences in body language and the interpretation of gestures.

Finally the sixth chapter will go into depth about an array of body language habits that people regularly display and how you should interpret them.

By the time you have read this book you should have a thorough understanding of the basis of body language, to help you improve and flourish in your relationships with other people.

# THE BASICS OF KINESICS

Body language, or kinesics as it is technically referred to, has been separated into five categories by social scientists. In this chapter learn about each of these five categories in turn.

## EMBLEMS

Emblems are signals that are 'concrete' and have a defined meaning in a certain culture or context. A thumbs up gesture is understood to communicate that everything is "ok" or that something went well.

Bear in mind that emblems are culturally sensitive however and that different regions in the world will have different meanings for the same emblems (covered in more detail in chapter 5).

Specific groups or subcultures may have their own emblems. It is not unusual for gangs or groups to develop their own emblems as a welcoming gestures or to show who is a member of the in-group. Think back to your school days – it is likely that you either had one of these emblems yourself or knew someone that did.

Alternatively people develop their own signals to communicate in social situations without other people understanding – such as secret 'sign language' or codes that children might use in school during lessons to not get the attention of the teachers.

## ILLUSTRATORS

Illustrators are gestures and movements that help convey and exaggerate what a person is saying. People commonly use illustrators when they are trying to describe something, moving their hands to signal shape, size or direction. Illustrators can also include pointing.

Bear in mind that illustrators are less consciously controlled than emblems. However, this nature can be used to help make inferences about other people. If someone is making a vast display with illustrators this often means they are highly engaged, but they may not have a huge degree of conscientiousness about their actions.

Conversely, if someone isn't displaying any illustrators they may not be engaged in the conversation at all or may not be enjoying it.

Illustrators can also often betray our true intents. If we are trying to say one thing, but we actually think or feel differently than our illustrators are one of main ways our body language can undermine us, as they can signal something different. Inconsistency between illustrators and our verbal communication, at the very least gives the impression of insincerity.

A common illustrator is often is a karate chop motion onto one open palm. This shows assertiveness and forcefulness. If someone displays this illustrator they often strong believe what they are saying, or they have a slightly aggressive slant.

Similarly, showing or tensing the knuckles often symbols aggression or a desire to be aggressive.

Not all illustrators are aggressive however! A raised palm and wagging finger for example, is often very condescending and in poor taste. It is used to signal that someone has made a mishap or done something wrong, but in a childish or lowly way. This illustrator should almost never be used as it will immediately turn people away from you.

Likewise, holding a palm over your heart is another illustrator that you need to carefully consider before using. It can be interpreted in the sense that you are being emotional and that what you are saying or listening to is heartfelt.

However, it can also come across as incredibly sarcastic, especially when apologizing or saying something that should be taken as sincere.

It is important to recognize how illustrators can be interpreted, especially as they are non-conscious – you may be turning people away from you or giving signals that you didn't intend to give (although these may display non-conscious feelings).

A full list of illustrators is likely to be rather more extensive then this guide can cover. However, try and start recognizing them in your daily life and whether you frequently display them (or whether people around you do).

## AFFECT DISPLAYS

In psychology, affect is a term used that means emotion. Hence, affect displays are emotional displays – movements that confer an emotional meaning.

This includes expressions, but also other aspects of kinesics. We tend to interpret people who are slouched or clinging to their own body with their arms as lacking in confidence or sad. Conversely, people who walk with a spring in their step or who bounce and are quite bodily animated when they talk as being happy. These are both examples of affect displays. Affect displays are often rather uncontrolled and spontaneous – as compared to emblems, which are used deliberately.

One common affect display is rubbing one's hands together. This is generally interpreted as a signal of excitement and anticipation. This movement actually serves a purpose however – it warms your hands together, which prepares them for action.

The intensity of this movement typically correlates to how powerful the emotion is felt – with faster rubbing motions, designating higher levels of anticipation.

Another affect display is rolling your sleeves up. This is another display that is preparing yourself for action – in this case, ensuring that your clothes don't get dirty or in the way of whatever you are trying to accomplish.

Affect displays are particularly hard to handle because they are one of the most spontaneous types of action. However, you can also learn about how they are portrayed and how to consider you should respond to them. If you make an aggressive affect display, you may want to make more passive or open displays which don't give out such aggressive impressions.

## REGULATORS

Regulators are nonverbal movements that help moderate what people are saying and the flow of conversation. Nodding or shaking one's head

for example, communicates agreement or disagreement, which helps

the other members of the conversation direct what they want to say.

Other regulators may include simply walking away (or starting to walk

away) or raising a finger (to gesture for silence).

Regulators tend to go unnoticed apart from the instances where they

are *not* being used. If there is a lack of regulators, it is painfully obvious

that they are not present. People interrupt each other, or one person

overtakes the conversation and overall the conversation does not flow

naturally.

If you find that you are one of these people that often interrupts other

people then perhaps you are not registering the regulators other people

are making.

Any signal that the other people in a conversation are impatient is a sign

that its probably your turn to stop talking, this may include fidgeting or

shuffling the body. Alternatively, it might include learning forward or

sitting with the mouth open (in preparation to speak). Other signals

might include people displaying illustrators or emblems, which also

signals that they are ready to communicate and that you might need to give them a chance to speak.

Similarly if people seem distracted or otherwise uninterested, perhaps you are not giving them enough opportunity to voice themselves. Overall, sometimes it is better just to prompt other people and listen, rather than feel the need to speak yourself, especially if you suspect your might inhibit conversation through not recognising regulators.

## ADAPTORS

Adaptors are behaviors that people employ, at low levels of self-awareness, which may indicate how they are feeling. To clarify, these include movements such as fiddling with one's hair, fidgeting with stationary, scratching at itches, bouncing on chairs, biting your lip (and so on).

Typically these actions are not interpreted as due to a conscious desire to perform a specific action, but rather as a habitual response. Adaptors are interesting because they do not have an intended meaning, but rather can be trigger by anxiety or stress. Adaptors are often developed in our younger years and can be increasingly displayed the more anxious we feel. Owing to the fact that they develop due to environmental conditions, adaptors can vary wildly between different people.

Adaptors can be useful in uncovering lies and moments of tension. If someone isn't telling you the truth – or is fabricating their story or account in some way (such as exaggerating) they tend to feel more anxious and stressed than normal. Therefore they may start to display adaptors and other signs of stress.

They may also highlight different parts of the conversation which are stress inducing. If you have mentioned a topic of conversation that makes other people uncomfortable for example, you might notice they start to produce adaptors.

However, they may also be entirely meaningless. Not everyone fidgets due to anxiety – sometimes people are uncomfortable for common sense reasons. Alternatively, some people have a tendency to fidget or otherwise move around. Be sure that you do not over-interpret!

# ACADEMIC FIELDS OF BODY LANGUAGE

Kinesics is the academic term for body language, but there is an entire spectrum of non-verbal communication each of which has their own field of study. In this chapter learn about the other types of non-verbal communication.

## MOTORICS

Motorics, as the name implies, is the study of movement in regards to communication. This includes the sub-groups of;

Mimics – movements of the face

Pantomimics – the movement/position of the entire body

Gesture – movements of the arms and hands

There the most important point to make here is that expressions (which fall under the category of mimics) are universal.

No matter where you are in the world and what culture you are talking to, all people will interpret an expression in the same way. This provides a useful basis for communication between people of different languages or origins – let your expressions speak for you!

# OCULESICS

Oculescis the study or use of eye movements in non-verbal communication.

Humans have a great ability in interpreting the eye movements of other humans. We can interpret a wandering gaze as a sign of distraction or lack of interest in the current conversation.

Direct eye contact can cause a feeling of intimacy or confidence and an avoidant gaze can imply insecurity or lack of confidence. Yet conversely, at times direct eye gaze can feel inappropriate or awkward.

Eye movement can also influence the flow and control of a conversation. Changes in eye movement can be used to signal a new event which requires attention or to direct people to where we are looking.

# HAPTICS

The study or use of physical touch in non-verbal communication.

The use of touch in non-verbal communication is incredibly complicated and nuanced. Touch can convey a vast range of emotions and intents, from playfulness to sexual attraction, to love & intimacy or even threat

& violence. Touch can also be part of social convention and ritual, such as a handshake or high five.

The use of touch also varies dramatically across cultures and countries. Even within western countries, friendly touch is more common and accepted within continental Europe, as opposed to in the U.K and U.S.

Touch also varies notably across genders. Studies suggest that men interpret being touched as different than woman and are more likely to respond negatively – potentially due to implications of dominance and submissiveness.

The main take-home point of touch is that it is a very emotional method of communication, often with a greater level of intensity than other methods. If touch is used in conjunction with language and non-verbal communication, it can emphasize and reinforce the impression you make. This is a double-edged sword however – if someone is uncomfortable with your presence, or perceives you negatively, touching them will likely strengthen this perception.

## PROXEMICS

The study and use of space in non-verbal communication. Proxemics interacts and influences haptics – you will need to be within a certain distance before touching even becomes appropriate.

If someone is standing 'too close' this can be interpreted as uncomfortable or inappropriate by the other person in the conversation. The appropriate level of closeness largely depends on the relationship between the two people involved. Study of proxemics has distinguished four approximate regions of space people can occupy in relation to another.

Intimate Distance – Less than 1.5ft

Personal Space - 1.5ft to 4ft

Social Space - 4ft to 12ft

Public Space – 12ft – 25ft

Intimate space is used for direct touch, embraces or whispering. Naturally intimate space conveys a strong and close relationship between the two people involved, often being lovers.

Personal space is typically for close friends and family. If other less familiar individuals enter this space, it is determined uncomfortable by the majority of people.

Social space is for acquaintances and other people who do not fall into the previous categories. This space is close enough to be considered reasonably engaged with the other person, but does not display any kind of intimacy or closeness.

The public space is often used for public speaking or group interactions. This is the upper bound for when conversations or verbal communication take place between people and groups.

## CHRONEMICS

The study and use of time in non-verbal communication. A fast tempo to a conversation can often be the result of anger or frustration, but it can also be as a result of engagement and excitement. Slower tempo can be the result of a lack of interest in both parties, but it can also imply that they are comfortable in each others presence. Slow tempo and pauses can often imply confidence.

Outside of conversation, the use of time also carries various connotations. In the western and east asian world, the use of time is called 'monochronic', which basically means precise or measured. Arriving exactly on time to an event is considered; being five, ten or any amount of time later is interpreted as rude (at least without reason).

Conversely, in other regions, such as Latin America or Africa, time usage is often called 'polychronic'. Broader time categories are used to signal events, such as 'morning', 'afternoon', 'dusk' and there is more wideness and variance for when a person can appear for events.

## PARALANGUAGE

The study and use of the voice in non-verbal communication. This may sound rather contradictory but paralanguage is actually hugely relevant. Psychology considers that a large factor in our communication are non-verbal (i.e not language based) aspects of our speech. This includes factors such as rhythm, intonation, speaking style and stress.

Think about your own experiences. You are more likely to engage with a person who is not speaking in a monotone and likewise, greater orators know how to alter and control the pace and emphasis of what they are saying for greater impact.

Similarly, if someones voice is cracking or shacking we will interpret what they are saying as being more emotional than if their voice were calm, even if they are saying the exact same message.

To improve your paralanguage, you will need to practice. Speakers typically train themselves by giving their speech or presentation in front of a full length mirror so they can see themselves whilst speaking. Likewise, it is common for speakers and orators to record their own speech so they can better analyze their speaking habits.

## BIPEDICS

The study and use of foot and leg gestures in non-verbal communication. Bipedics is a relatively new addition to the other categories, with far less research on how influential it is. Nonetheless, be aware of its existence! You may hear of bipedics in the future!

As you can see, there are a lot of categories! Many of these categories overlap or cover the same conceptual space – bipedics (movement of the legs & feet) for example, can be interpreted as a sub-group of motirics (movement). Similarly, the categories mentioned in chapter 1 will also fit into the categories (emblems for example are a type of *gesture)*.

It's not crucial to appreciate the exact categorizations, but they can give you a great lead for further research and well as the striking variety of body language signals that people actually consider. Chances are, before reading this chapter you were not aware that bipedics – or the body language of the legs and hips – was a scientific field of its own accord!

Yet now you know that even your legs can give influence how you are portrayed.

# IMPROVING NON-VERBAL COMMUNICATION

Now that you are familiar with the theory and definitions regarding non-verbal communication, it's time to put this knowledge to work. This chapter covers how to actually improve your non-verbal communication skills.

One of the key points to remember is that you still need to be genuine and honest when influencing your body language. Use the knowledge you have compiled to develop self-awareness and understanding of the people around you. Utilizing this self-awareness, you can then selectively emphasize parts of your communication for greater effect.

The point being made is that body language is not magical and will not be able to utterly transform how you are perceived. If you try to 'fake' your body language, it can cause yourself to feel stressed as well as produce inconsistent signals, which can counteract whatever effect you are attempting to produce, especially if you are not well practiced.

Always start by being self-aware of your habits. Once you are familiar with your habits, slightly adjust them when appropriate. The better you become at recognizing and changing your body language, the more you can influence it. You should work your way up to the deep end, rather than jumping in straight away!

With this in mind, consider what you want to achieve whenever you are manipulating your body language. Theorists have argued non-verbal communication can lead to the following outcomes:

*Repetition* – Emphasizes and reinforces the message you are saying verbally

*Contradiction* – Undermines or counteract the message you are saying verbally

*Substitution* – Used in place of a verbal message (often for more effect)

*Complementing* – Also reinforces and emphasizes verbal communication, but in a slightly different manner to repetition. Complementing adds emotional impact.

*Accenting* – Reinforcement that changes how the message is perceived. Hitting the wall as you speak will give your message a much more aggressive implication, for example.

Be aware of these roles and consider what area you may be looking to improve upon. If people do not seem to take well to you, you may have a habit of contradicting your verbal behaviors with non-verbal communication.

Failing to manage eye contact, or holding an uncomfortable body posture will almost always lead people to be uncomfortable in your presence, even if you are otherwise pleasant, interesting or funny.

Conversely, a lack of accenting or repetition can mean that your speeches or goal based communications do not garner the impact they deserve.

The general rule here is to be aware of inconsistencies between what you are saying and how your body language is portraying you.

When looking for these inconsistencies, however, it is important to look for trends. Body language is incredibly rich and nuanced; over-interpreting and analyzing every aspect will made your head spin. Instead, look for groups of signals and signs that are persistently and strongly presented. These tend to underlie stronger feelings.

Likewise, be aware of you own potential to misread other people's body language. It's fine to pick up on the signals of other people and respond accordingly, but at the end of the day, every situation is ambiguous. It is often best to not to take most signals you perceive too much to heart, especially if they are infrequent.

Next, rely upon your instinctual feelings. Humans are social animals and nearly all of us, by default, will have a strong understanding of body language, even if we are not explicitly aware of the fact. Our ability to control our body language, or be aware of it in the first place, is our main failing when it comes to communication.

Additionally, you need to learn to deal with and manage stress. Our body language is often compromised due to the negative emotions that we encounter in social situations, such as stress or anxiety. These emotions are often about our own personal state of mind, rather than the world or the people around us. Nonetheless, they influence how other people perceive us and therefore how they interact with us.

Ultimately, there is a self-fulfilling relationship between negative body language and negative interactions with other people. Our ability to control our body language is limited, so often it is more advantageous to manage the stress and anxiety that are causing the negative body language to begin with. In this sense, it is important to treat the cause, rather than the symptoms.

Furthermore, stress and anxiety also influence how we interpret the body language of other people. When we are feeling stressed or anxious, we are more likely to misinterpret the body language of other people, often in a negatively biased way.

Simply put, stress and anxiety compromise our body language in a myriad of ways and must be dealt with before body language can be improved.

Additionally, one more way you can improve is to simply ask people who you are close to how you are perceived when you communicate. Sometimes you may perceive yourself as being portrayed worse than your body language actually implies.

Alternatively you may be ignorant of one persistent aspect or habit of your body language that is creating a huge amount of impact. Using close friends and family members to ask for feedback is a great way to compensate for a lack of self-awareness of your own body language.

Moreover don't be afraid to occasionally clarify what you think other people are attempting to communicate. We are often embarrassed or too shy to ask for a clarification in a social setting, yet it is often necessary. Furthermore asking for clarifications also helps develop your body language interpretation.

Another pointer to consider is the context of a given situation. Humans have an almost psychic ability to infer how another person may be feeling, if we take the time to think through the situations they are in. Perhaps their body language is aggressive because they had a bad day at work and they are stressed, rather than any relationship concerns with you.

# The Infamous 'First Impression'

You've probably heard the popular psychology claim that the first impression we make with a new person has huge implications for how that person will perceive us in the future.

Whilst the claims are highly exaggerated, the basis is true; first impressions are vital to how we are considered, especially for acquaintances. For example, a study performed by Malcom Gladwell, found that speed daters made up their mind on whether they were compatible for each other in the first 10 seconds of meeting.

In this chapter learn how to nail the dreaded first impression to ensure that your relationships start in the right way.

First impressions are largely based on factors which you have limited control over. Factors such as age, sex or attractiveness will be judged quickly, and unconsciously, often before you have even spoken. Therefore, if you truly want to maximize your first impression then you need to control the shallow factors first.

This means that you are appropriately dressed for whatever occasion you are in, as well as appropriately groomed. Obviously the convention will be different in different situations, but the intensity of judgments may also vary. Arriving to an interview in casual dress is a significant failure in determining what to wear than going to a social situation slightly overdressed.

Once you have these factors arranged to the best of your ability you can then consider the other psychological factors that you may be able to influence. Current research suggests there are two 'domains' in which we are judged during our first impressions. These domains are continuum's in which we are placed and this rough value will be used to interpret our later behavior.

The first domain is trustworthiness. This factor appears to largely depend on signals and signs that suggest we are happy or angry (which the latter suggesting we are less trustworthy).

This follows conventional advice to introduce yourself with a smile and be pleasant and warm to people when you first talk to them. This gives the impression of happiness, which bizarrely, may be important more important than trustworthiness itself when being judged on trustworthiness.

The second domain is dominance. Dominance, at least on first glance, is largely based upon facial maturity and masculine features.

Dominance is a tricky factor to consider because it is more ambiguous than trustworthiness. We all desire to be perceived as trustworthy, but we may desire to be perceived as dominant or non-dominant depending on the situation. At the very least, we do not want to appear submissive.

If we are judged to be highly dominant, our later behavior can be judged as aggressive rather than merely confident.

Obviously your facial profile and bodily maturity cannot be influenced. However, factors such as body posture and the gestures you may can influence judgments of dominance. Open and relaxed posturing is more likely to be perceived as dominant than hunched or closed postures. Likewise, leaning forward or handing a firm (but not bone-breaking) handshake are all factors that dictate dominance. These details will be covered in more depth in Chapter 6.

# CULTURAL DIFFERENCES

Some aspects of our body language and non-verbal communication are universal, such as our expressions. Other aspects, in particular *gestures* or *emblems* are very culturally-sensitive. This can lead to huge misunderstandings between people of different cultures. In this chapter learn how some common western gestures may be interpreted differently in other regions of the world.

For example, in the West it is common to use a beckoning gesture to draw people towards you from a distance. This gesture usually involves raising an arm out in front of the body and curling one or more fingers to the palm, signaling that another person should come to your presence.

However, in many Asian cultures, this gesture is highly offensive, as this gesture is related to beckoning dogs. Therefore the usage of that particular gesture is tantamount to calling the other person a dog or hound, which is also a highly sensitive insult in many Asian regions.

Similarly, pointing, which is simply used to direct attention in most Western cultures can be considered offensive in many Asian regions.

Instead, raising a hand vertically towards what you want to draw attention to is considered more appropriate.

Winking is a facial movement that highly varies between cultures, and even individuals. Winking is often used playfully in the West, or to communicate an underlying shared knowledge is a social setting. In Latin American, winking is a more sexualized, and is used almost exclusively in that sense. Conversely, in China, winking is often seen as rude altogether.

The 'ok' emblem is also interpreted differently in different regions of the world. In Japan, the gesture looks similar to a Japanese coin, and therefore the emblem typically refers to money. In Southern Europe, the Mediterranean and Northern Africa, the same emblem means zero or nothing.

In many middle eastern and Latin American cultures, it is considered more appropriate to stand closer to one another, even in regards to strangers and lesser known acquaintances. Muslim cultures, in general, are much more sensitive with proximity between men and women, however.

Eye contact also varies dramatically between cultures. In some Asian cultures, it is often a sign of disrespect to make eye contact before being familiar with the other person. Especially when a younger person attempts to make eye contact with an older person.

On the same vein, sitting with poor posture is often considered to be disrespectful in many places – signifying a lack of interest or attention.

Ultimately, you cannot learn every custom or cultural twist on a gesture or an emblem. However, being aware if the potential differences between cultural gestures can help you avoid an embarrassing mistake. Rely upon verbal communication whenever you can and be forthcoming with your expression (which are more universally understood).

# INTERPRETING INDIVIDUAL SIGNALS

As of yet we have most talked about interpreting signals you are probably already aware of. Most of us do not need to be old that slouching implies a lack of confidence, or that shouting implies aggressiveness. Yet there are ranges of smaller signals that are less well understood. This chapter will help you better understand these micro signals.

## THE HEAD

The head is one of the key features of body language. We often focus on the face but fail to recognize the overall position of the head. Biology and evolution have taught us to guard our heads, above and beyond all of the other organs of our body. Therefore, if we feel threatened, unsafe or otherwise uneasy, we have a tendency to pull and lift our heads backwards.

It is only when we feel safe and engaged that we will push our heads forward, or if we are looking to fight with another person.

Therefore, you should interpret a forwardness of the head as *action* taking or *aggressive*, whilst a lean back of the head is *defensive* or *passive.*

This can have implications that you might not anticipate. Leaning your head backwards when your being told a story for example, doesn't just imply that your not engaged, it also implies that you don't believe the story itself (or believe it is exaggerated).

Tilting the head to the side can be a general display of interest or empathy, but this particular habit varies dramatically between people.

## HEAD NODDING

We all know that nodding the head implies agreement. However, depending on the frequency and style of nodding, this agreement can be genuine, false or something else entirely.

Nodding is an example of a mirrored behavior – it is a common behavior that people employ to feel accepted or similar to each other. When a person nods during conversation it increases the likelihood that the other people in the conversation will also nod.

What this also means, is that nodding often becomes a unconscious or sub-conscious action that actually has little value on whether a person agrees or not with your topic of conversation.

However, it does almost always imply a sense of good will and connection to the other person. If you start nodding during a conversation but the other person doesn't, this often implies that they don't understand, that they don't agree or simply they don't like you or your topic of conversation.

Test this on your friends or family. Try gently nodding during your conversation and see whether the other person reciprocates. There is a high chance that those you like will start nodding, unconsciously, in return. Of course, do not read too much into this — it may be the case that the other person is highly conscientious of their own actions and doesn't have a tendency to nod. Likewise, if a person is used to appearing agreeable, such as those who work in customer service, they may also tend to defer to nodding in general.

Yet you also have to pay attention on the speed and the overall rhythm of the nod. A gentle, slow nod often is often associated with strong agreement, but also with a genuine interest in the conversation. This nod means that the person is enjoying the conversation and is happy for it to progress as it's a natural pace.

Conversely, a fast rapid nod, especially if combined with adaptors or any kind of fidgeting is often a signal that the other person is impatient. They may simply be waiting for their turn in the conversation or for you to stop beating around the bush and make your point. This nod may not actually imply agreement or engagement, but rather them attempting to placate you until they get their turn in conversation.

In between these two nods is a more moderately based nod. This nod is often slightly more deliberate and focused. It tends to imply the other person is engaged and has a good will and attempting to bond or link with you.

Furthermore, also consider whether people who are nodding are looking towards you or away from you. If they are looking away from you. If they are not looking towards you, it can imply distraction and reinforce that they are simply trying to placate you. Alternatively, it can mean that they are pondering your words. People don't maintain direct focus or eye contact all of the time, and they might need a small moment to digest what you are saying.

Also consider, upwards head nods. Upwards nods can be used to signal recognition – they are often used when a person sees another person. They tend to appear more casual and less engaged, so they tend to be employed by people who wish to display a distant.

## HEAD SHAKE

A shake of the head from side to side generally signals 'no'. Yet there are small variants on how this should be interpreted. A quick, regular head shake implies strong and potent disagreement. This is used in circumstances when the person couldn't disagree more with what you are saying.

A very slow but paced head shake often tends to imply disbelief. This is displayed in circumstances where the other person just outright cannot believe what has been said. It is often associated with denial of what has been said, though this is not always the case.

A gentler, but unstable head nod is often associated with misunderstanding. Think of this as communicating, 'no I don't understand' rather than an outright disagreement or disbelief.

The important point to raise about the head shake is that is often subtle. People attempt to avoid appearing like a caricature, which means they tend to downplay these body language signals. Therefore you need to be particularly attentive when recognizing these signals, especially if you are trying to convince the other person of something.

## AVERSION

A head nod can imply agreement or a headshake can imply disagreement. Yet one of the most dramatic and strongest head movements is when the head is turned away from the conversation or the other person altogether. Think of how people may react when they are disgusted – they often hunch up and turn away from what disgusts them. This is a similar type of movement.

A full turn-away is a very cold movement, but it still has its own stages. Turning the head away is understood to be less powerful than turning the entire shoulder away. Turning your entire back to someone is one of the coldest movements altogether.

As with all body language movements, this can be misinterpreted for similar body language positions, which mean other things. It is not unusual for someone to look into the distance when they are thinking about a topic of conversation – this isn't the same thing as aversion.

However, if this is accompanied by a lack of responsiveness in the conversation or an overall sign of impatience, then this implies an aversive response.

## VULNERABILITY & DOMINANCE

Just with our head, our torso is also a vulnerable section of the body, which contains major organs, such as the heart and the lungs. The same evolutionary principles that apply to our head, therefore, also apply to our torso which influences our overall body language. When we feel comfortable, safe and confident we are happy to expose your torso and lean forward. Likewise, when we feel insecure or lack confidence we hide the torso or shield it with our arms.

You should recognize such displays from people in your life. Bosses and other people in management positions also typically adopt wide, open postures with their torso's unobstructed – a display of confidence and security, even in the workplace or stressful situations.

Resting on your hands on your hips is another display of dominance.

Conversely, it is common for those who are depressed or anxious to feel the need to cover up.

This body language also however relates to we feel dominant and in control of our situation. By leaving your vulnerable sections of your body exposed, this has a strange level of power. It implies that although you are vulnerable, no-one will attack you – which generates even more confidence.

It's stems from the assumption that if there were a conflict, you would win. Hence there is no need to shield the body and the vulnerable positions are also the most dominant.

Although we live in a far more sophisticated environment than the one we evolved from, these simple dominance-related factors still apply.

However, vulnerability doesn't always correlate with dominance. Sometimes vulnerable positions also imply intimacy and trust between the two individuals involved – that an attack or an exploitation of said vulnerability will not occur (therefore it is okay to be vulnerable).

## SEXUAL BODY LANGUAGE

Naturally, we alter our body language depending on who we are attracted to and what impression we want to give to the opposite sex.

Opening or widening the legs often shows attraction, or confidence in a sexual display, which is frequent in young men. Conversely, crossing the legs or holding the palms over this area shows vulnerability, innocence and shyness.

However, often how open our legs are is more a matter of comfort, especially on hot days!  Watch out for legs being opened and an overall display of the crotch region in conjunction with other signals of dominance and confidence, especially in men, if you want to interpret greater levels of meaning.

# CONCLUSION

Body language is fascinating. It provides a deep layer of communication between two people, displaying signals and signs that words cannot.

We all want to manage how we are perceived at times and what other people think of us, yet we are susceptible to being 'read' through habits that we are not taught to control. Furthermore, we want to read other people better, both to improve our relationships but also, at times, for more self-serving purposes. Achieving the respect from your colleagues at work or nailing that sales pitch requires an intricate knowledge of body language and how to manipulate it.

Yet, what is most interesting of all, is that most of us already have a strong in-built sense of body language. Everyday we respond and interpret this body language, even on a non-conscious level. When we nod our heads in agreement to what someone else is saying or feel uncomfortable around someone who is fidgeting, we are tuning into this body language and acting appropriately.

This guide has aimed itself at helping you make this innate understanding of body language, explicit. By having this guide you should now be aware of the numerous ways in which we display tiny, but significant behaviors that demonstrate what we think or how we feel. Whether it is simply understanding the evolutionary perspective on dominance and vulnerability, recognizing how the different layers of head nods or understanding what gestures are aggressive, this guide has provided you with our modern understanding of body language.

In the first chapter of this book, you learned about the fivefold categorization of body language; emblems, illustrators, adaptors, affect displays and regulators. You know what purpose each of these body language serves and common examples of each of them.

In the second chapter you were informed about the different fields and disciplines within the topic of body language. You now know that haptics is the study of touch in communication or that chronemics is the study of time in communication.

The third chapter taught you a wealth of ways in which you can use to improve your non-verbal communication. These include, but are not limited to; being mindful of your body language and the language of other people around you, managing stress and anxiety, interpreting persistent & groups of signals and looking for body language -verbal communication inconsistencies.

The fourth chapter give you some insight in how to develop a great first impression, teaching you about factors such as appearance and the trustworthiness dimension.

The fifth chapter provided you with awareness of how body language varies between regions and cultures. You now know to be slightly wary when using gestures and emblems in different parts of the world, as well as appreciating the universalness of expressions.

Finally, the sixth chapter delved deep into individual aspects of body language such as head nodding, shaking, vulnerability, dominance and much more. You should understand *why* these body language signals are displayed, the small variances between similar types of body language and what to watch out for when you are communicating with others.

By having finished this guide, you should now be ready to bring a new level of awareness and mindfulness into your interactions with other people. Learn from the other people around you and sharpen your sense of interpreting what people are thinking and feeling.

Once you are familiar and skilled at this art, manipulating and refining your own body language will naturally flow. Before you know it, you will be a master of communication and impressions, reading people around you at ease and sending all the right signals.

Deep down, this is what many of us want to achieve, in our work place or unfamiliar social settings as well as our relationships that are not quite where we want them to be. It's now down to you to put your knowledge to the test. Good luck!

# Message from the author

## Thank you!

Please check out my author page on Amazon to see my latest publications. Please don't forget to **download your Free Gift!**

Once again I want to thank you for reading my book. I really hope you got a lot out of it.

If you enjoyed this book I would really appreciate it if you could leave me a positive review on Amazon. You can **click here** to go directly to the book on Amazon and leave your review.

I love getting feedback from my readers and reviews on Amazon really do make a difference. I read all my reviews and would really appreciate your thoughts.

Thanks so much.

Scott Colter

# OTHER BOOKS BY THE AUTHOR

Psychology: *Conquer the battles of your mind with powerful techniques to overcome stress, anxiety & Negative Thinking*

# Free Gift

**Drop the Fat Now!**
**Natural Solutions to Getting Trim**

>>Click Here To Download "Drop the Fat Now" for FREE<<

Made in the USA
Middletown, DE
09 March 2016